Art Hoax

Ari Lun

Illustrated by Geoff Todd

ISBN 978-0-646-83515-0
Published by Geoff Todd Off The Wall
65 Queen Street, Ararat, Victoria, Australia 3377
Copyright © Geoff Todd, 2021

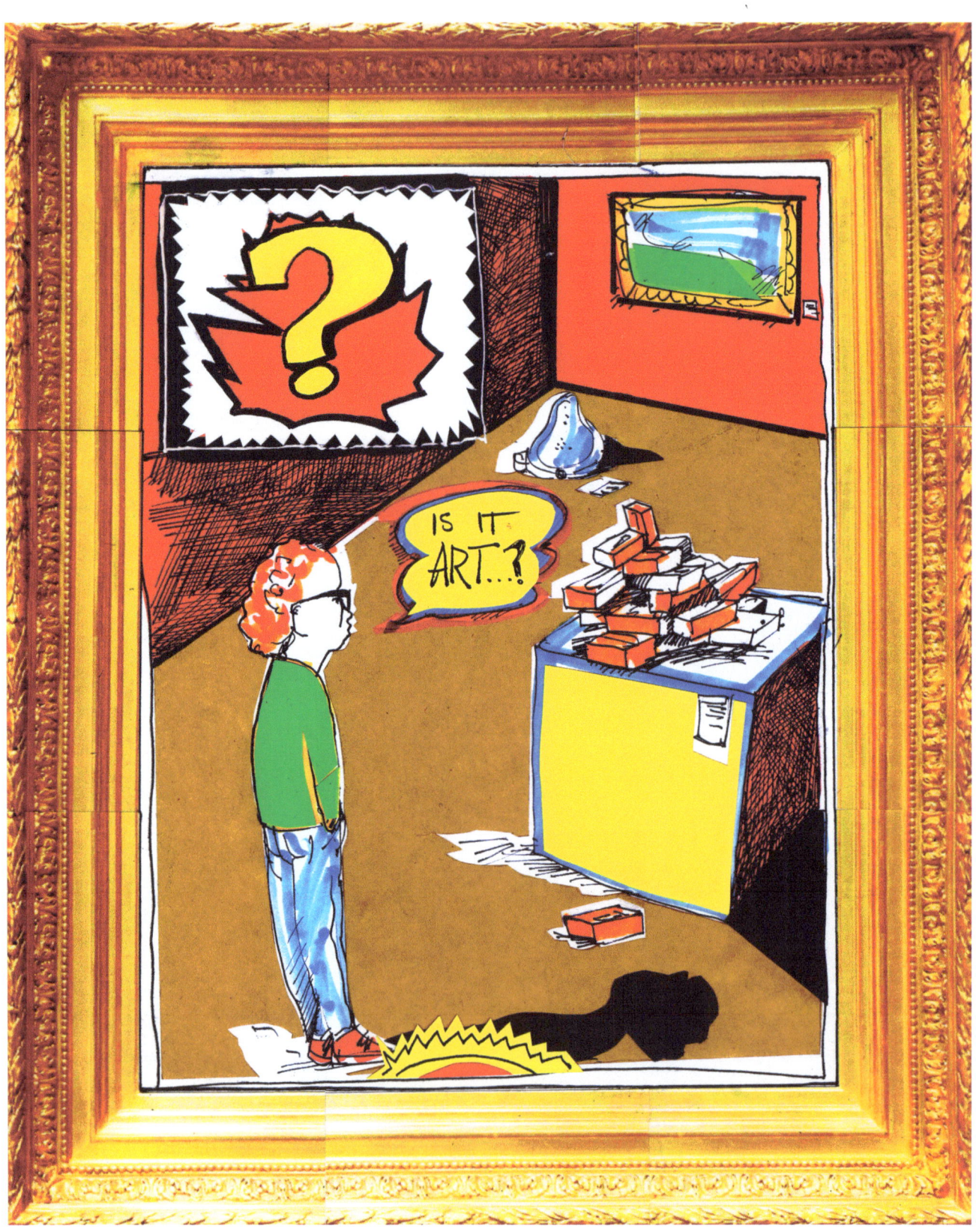

FOREWORD

Art Hoax is written for anybody who might wonder why unlikely objects in today's world are called art and sometimes valued at extraordinarily high worth.

This is an honest argument claiming the world has been duped by dealers in art, art galleries, art museums and on occasions, even artists.

Presented here from hand cut and pasted original collages by Geoff Todd, *Art Hoax* proposes that the evidence of the artist's hand in art is not something to hide, nor something to cause embarrassment, but rather something of which to be proud.

All quotations are from real people – living or dead – and attributions to any quotations are within the text for the sceptics and academics who might wish to verify them. The argument is very short, as is this foreword, so readers who are not interested in a large tome arguing points of aesthetics, art and concept, may find this book as an alternative half-hour read, which will equip them for an exciting dinner table debate.

I. P. Rossi
2020

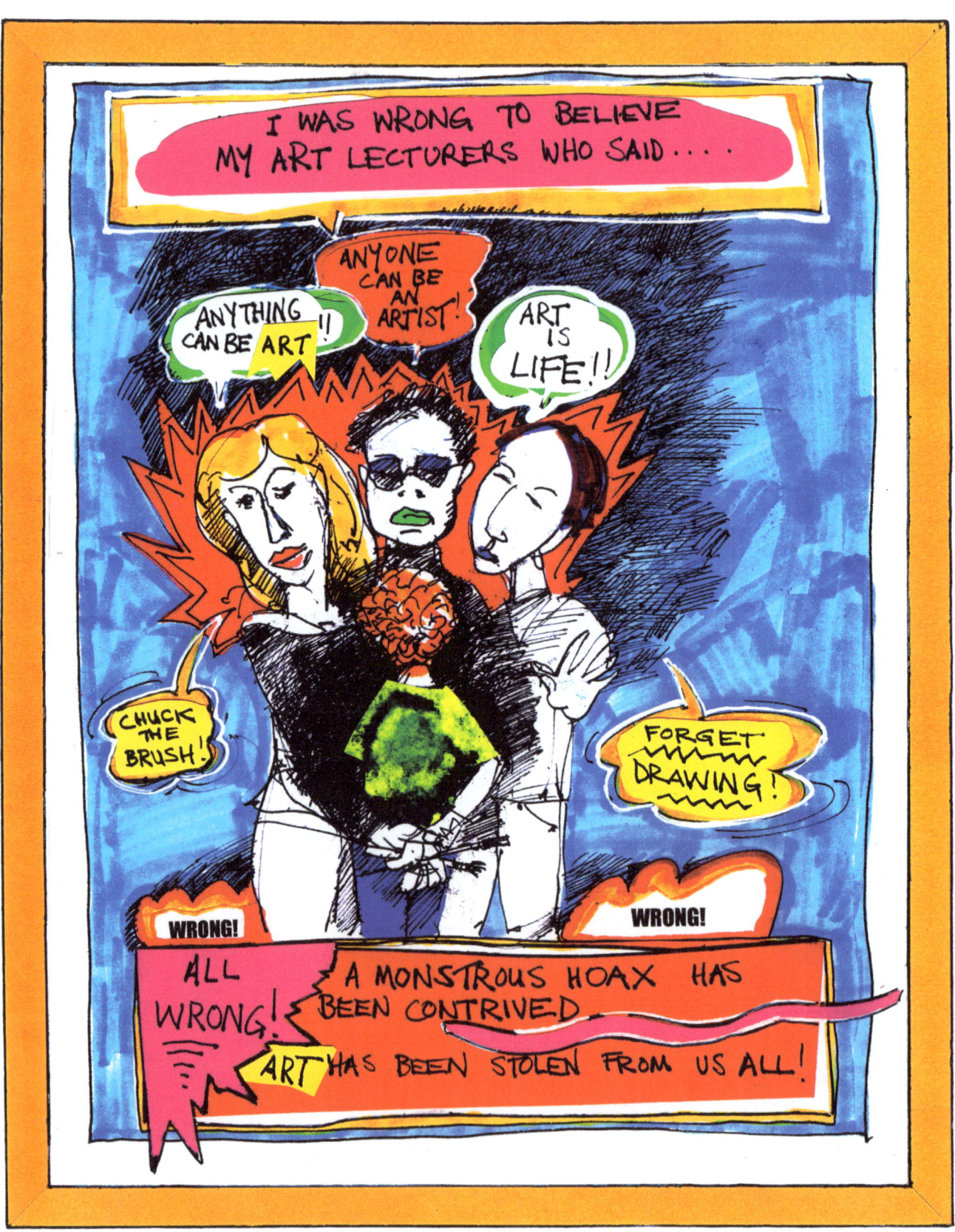

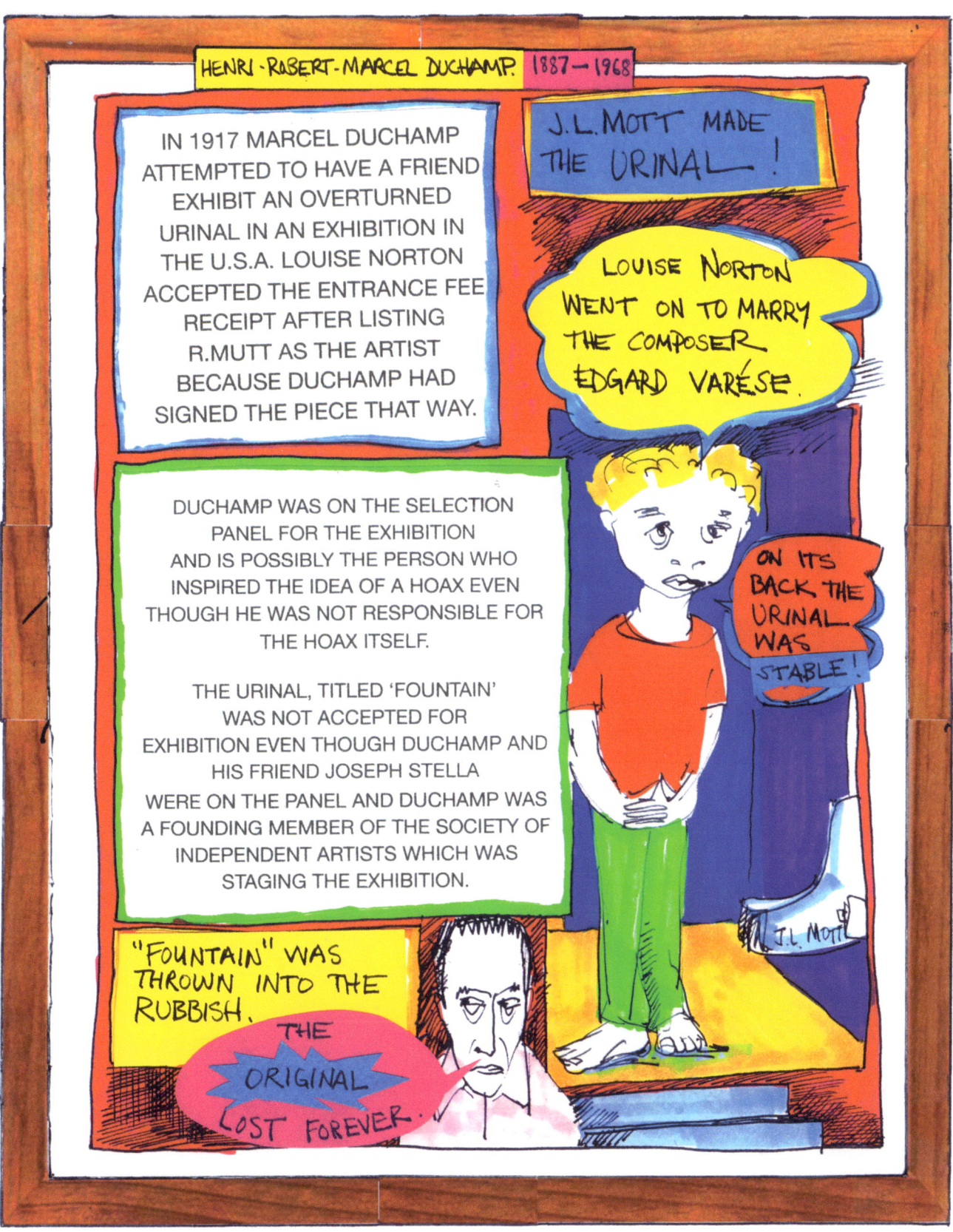

HENRI·ROBERT·MARCEL DUCHAMP. 1887—1968

IN 1917 MARCEL DUCHAMP ATTEMPTED TO HAVE A FRIEND EXHIBIT AN OVERTURNED URINAL IN AN EXHIBITION IN THE U.S.A. LOUISE NORTON ACCEPTED THE ENTRANCE FEE RECEIPT AFTER LISTING R.MUTT AS THE ARTIST BECAUSE DUCHAMP HAD SIGNED THE PIECE THAT WAY.

J.L.MOTT MADE THE URINAL.!

LOUISE NORTON WENT ON TO MARRY THE COMPOSER EDGARD VARÉSE.

DUCHAMP WAS ON THE SELECTION PANEL FOR THE EXHIBITION AND IS POSSIBLY THE PERSON WHO INSPIRED THE IDEA OF A HOAX EVEN THOUGH HE WAS NOT RESPONSIBLE FOR THE HOAX ITSELF.

THE URINAL, TITLED 'FOUNTAIN' WAS NOT ACCEPTED FOR EXHIBITION EVEN THOUGH DUCHAMP AND HIS FRIEND JOSEPH STELLA WERE ON THE PANEL AND DUCHAMP WAS A FOUNDING MEMBER OF THE SOCIETY OF INDEPENDENT ARTISTS WHICH WAS STAGING THE EXHIBITION.

ON ITS BACK THE URINAL WAS STABLE!

"FOUNTAIN" WAS THROWN INTO THE RUBBISH. THE ORIGINAL LOST FOREVER.

J.L. MOTT

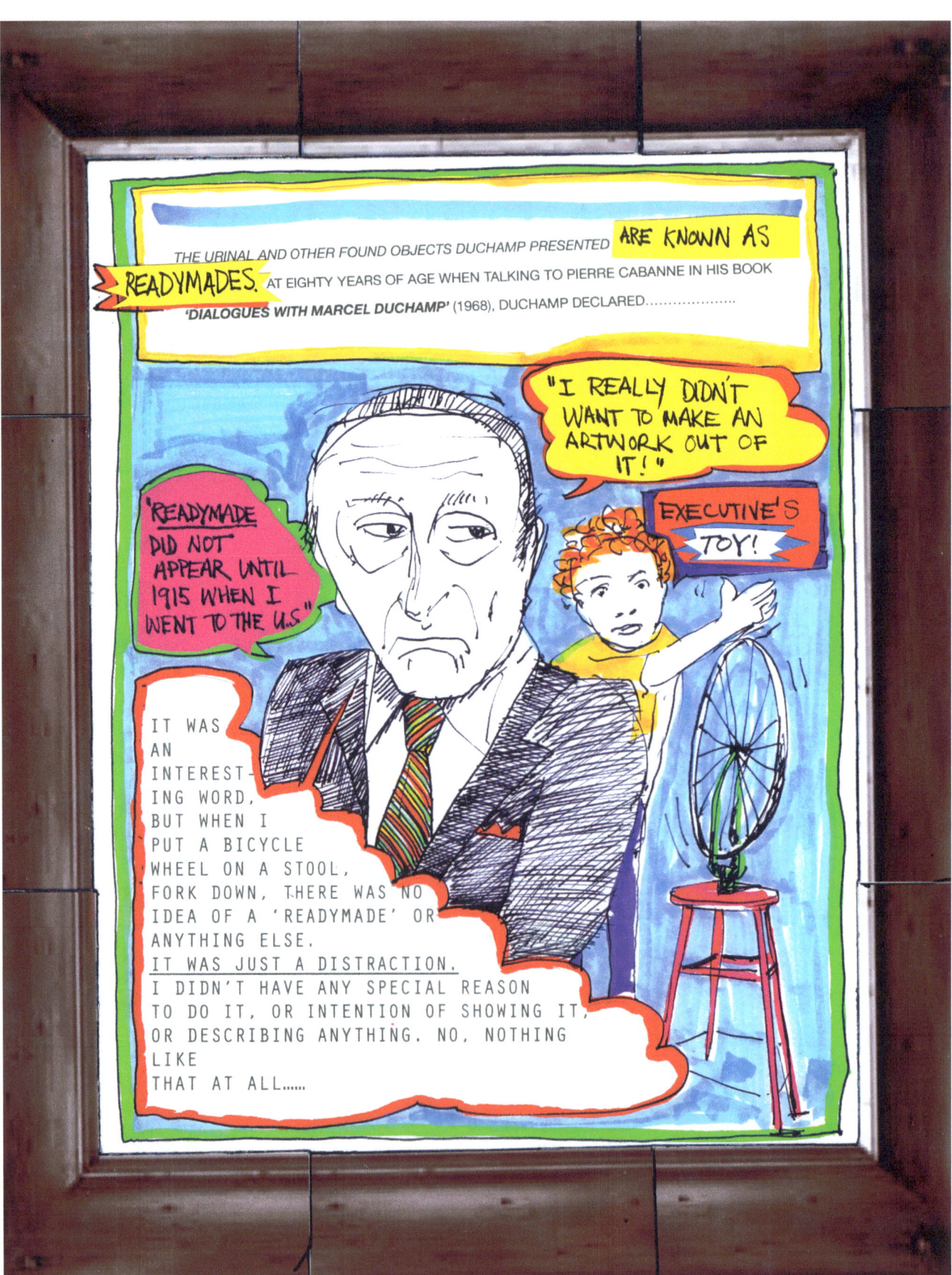

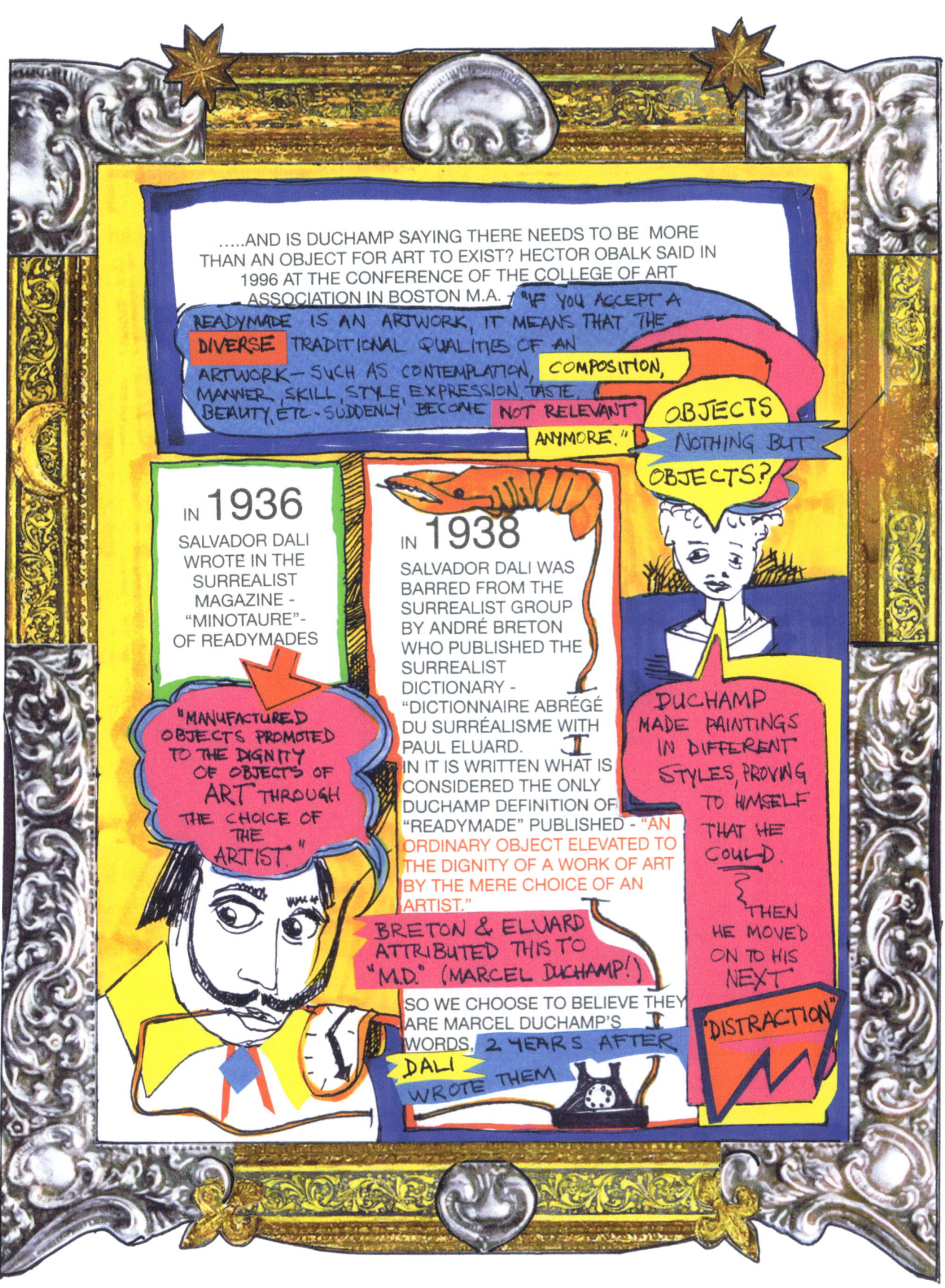

.....AND IS DUCHAMP SAYING THERE NEEDS TO BE MORE THAN AN OBJECT FOR ART TO EXIST? HECTOR OBALK SAID IN 1996 AT THE CONFERENCE OF THE COLLEGE OF ART ASSOCIATION IN BOSTON M.A. - "IF YOU ACCEPT A READYMADE IS AN ARTWORK, IT MEANS THAT THE DIVERSE TRADITIONAL QUALITIES OF AN ARTWORK- SUCH AS CONTEMPLATION, COMPOSITION, MANNER, SKILL, STYLE, EXPRESSION, TASTE, BEAUTY, ETC - SUDDENLY BECOME NOT RELEVANT ANYMORE."

OBJECTS NOTHING BUT OBJECTS?

IN 1936 SALVADOR DALI WROTE IN THE SURREALIST MAGAZINE - "MINOTAURE"- OF READYMADES

"MANUFACTURED OBJECTS PROMOTED TO THE DIGNITY OF OBJECTS OF ART THROUGH THE CHOICE OF THE ARTIST."

IN 1938 SALVADOR DALI WAS BARRED FROM THE SURREALIST GROUP BY ANDRÉ BRETON WHO PUBLISHED THE SURREALIST DICTIONARY - "DICTIONNAIRE ABRÉGÉ DU SURRÉALISME WITH PAUL ELUARD. IN IT IS WRITTEN WHAT IS CONSIDERED THE ONLY DUCHAMP DEFINITION OF "READYMADE" PUBLISHED - "AN ORDINARY OBJECT ELEVATED TO THE DIGNITY OF A WORK OF ART BY THE MERE CHOICE OF AN ARTIST."

BRETON & ELUARD ATTRIBUTED THIS TO "M.D." (MARCEL DUCHAMP!)

SO WE CHOOSE TO BELIEVE THEY ARE MARCEL DUCHAMP'S WORDS, 2 YEARS AFTER DALI WROTE THEM

DUCHAMP MADE PAINTINGS IN DIFFERENT STYLES, PROVING TO HIMSELF THAT HE COULD. THEN HE MOVED ON TO HIS NEXT "DISTRACTION"

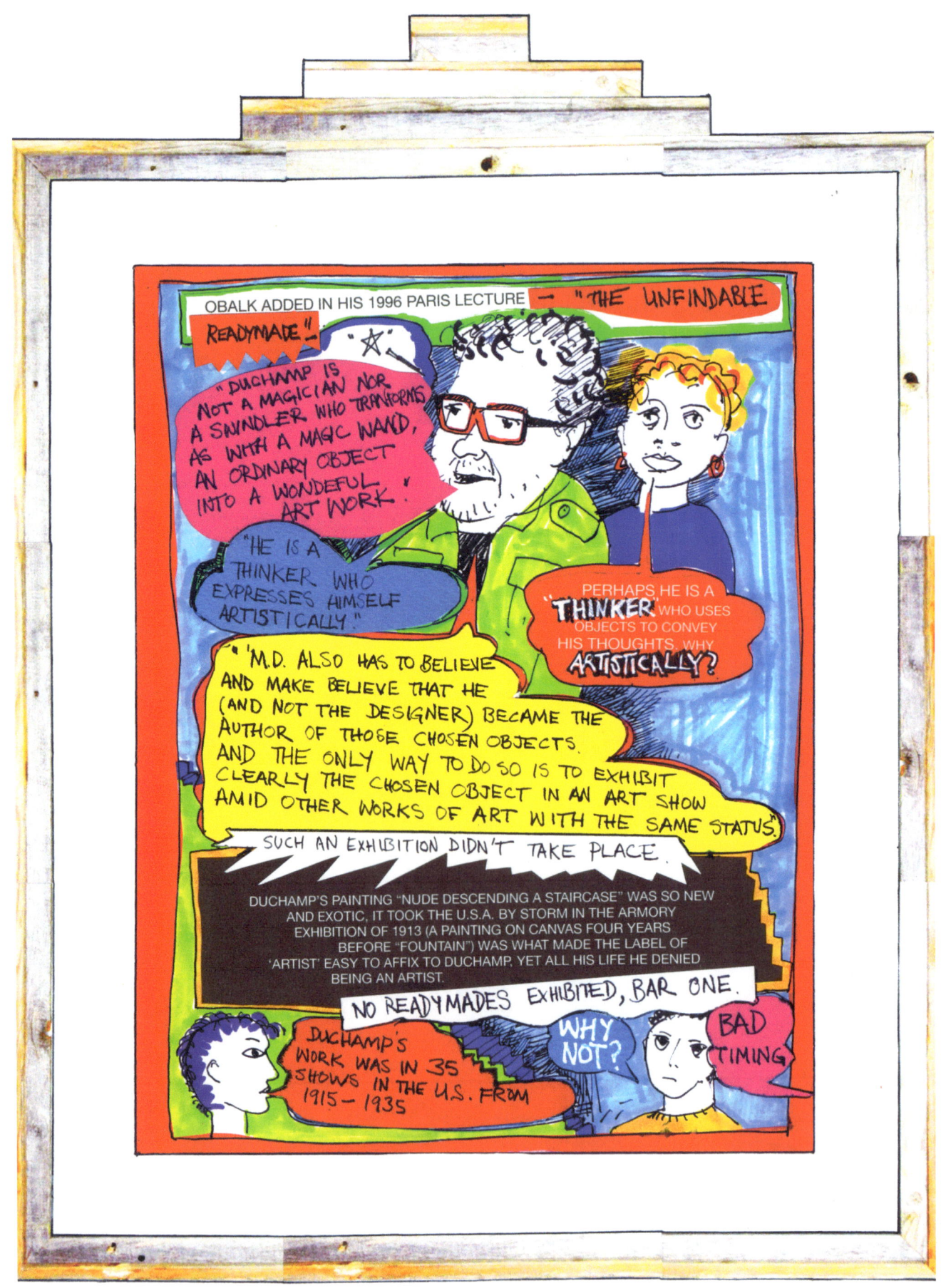

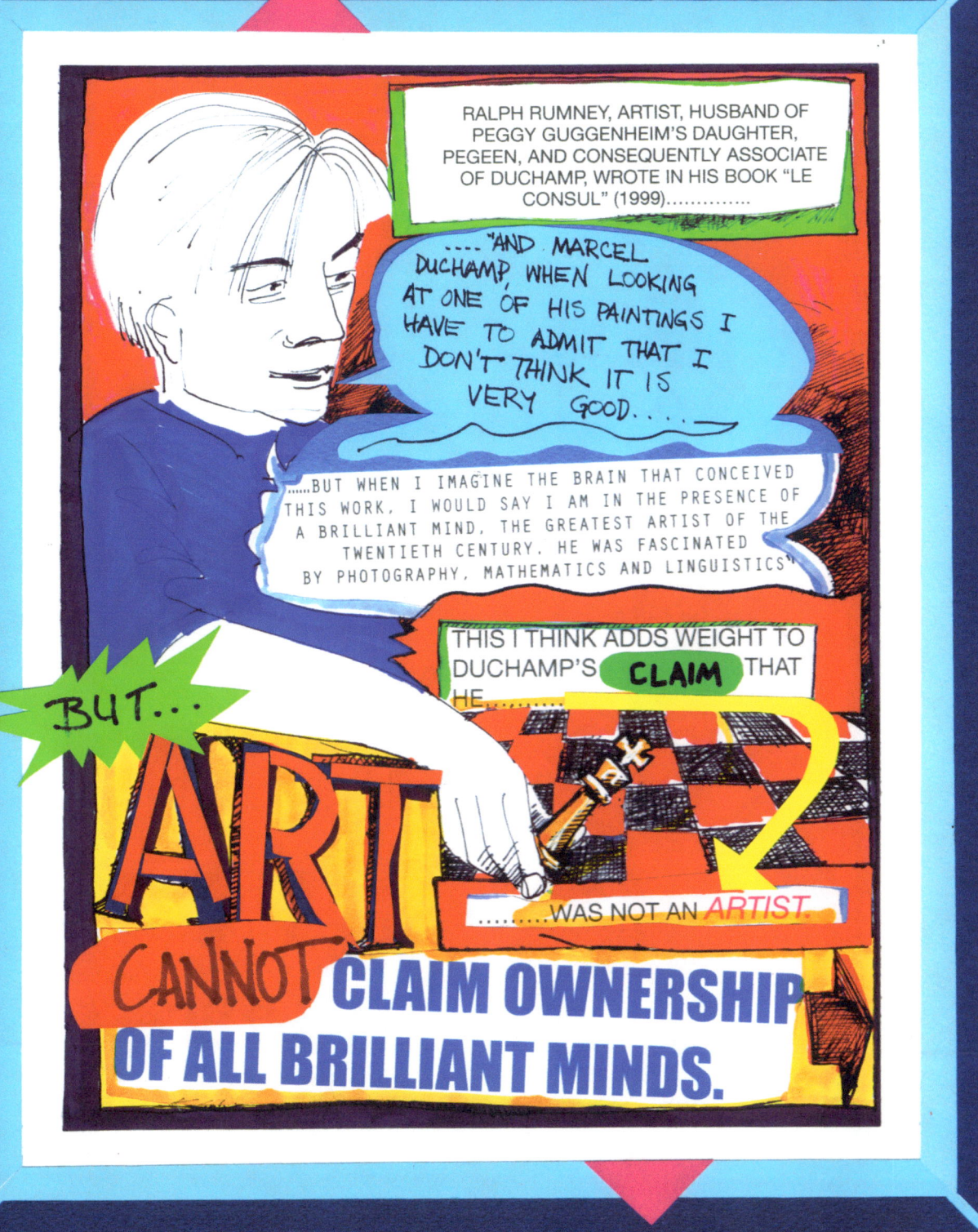

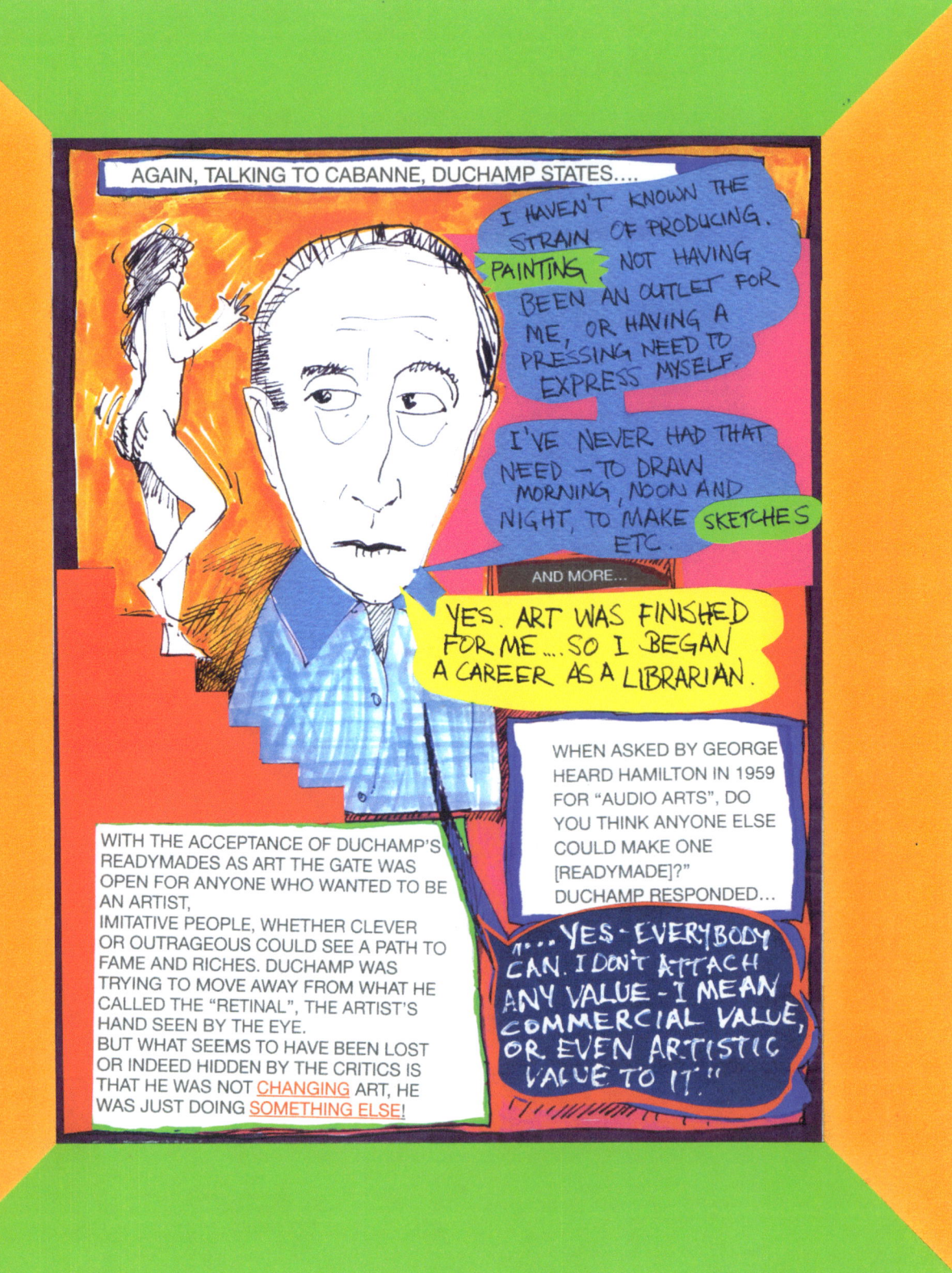

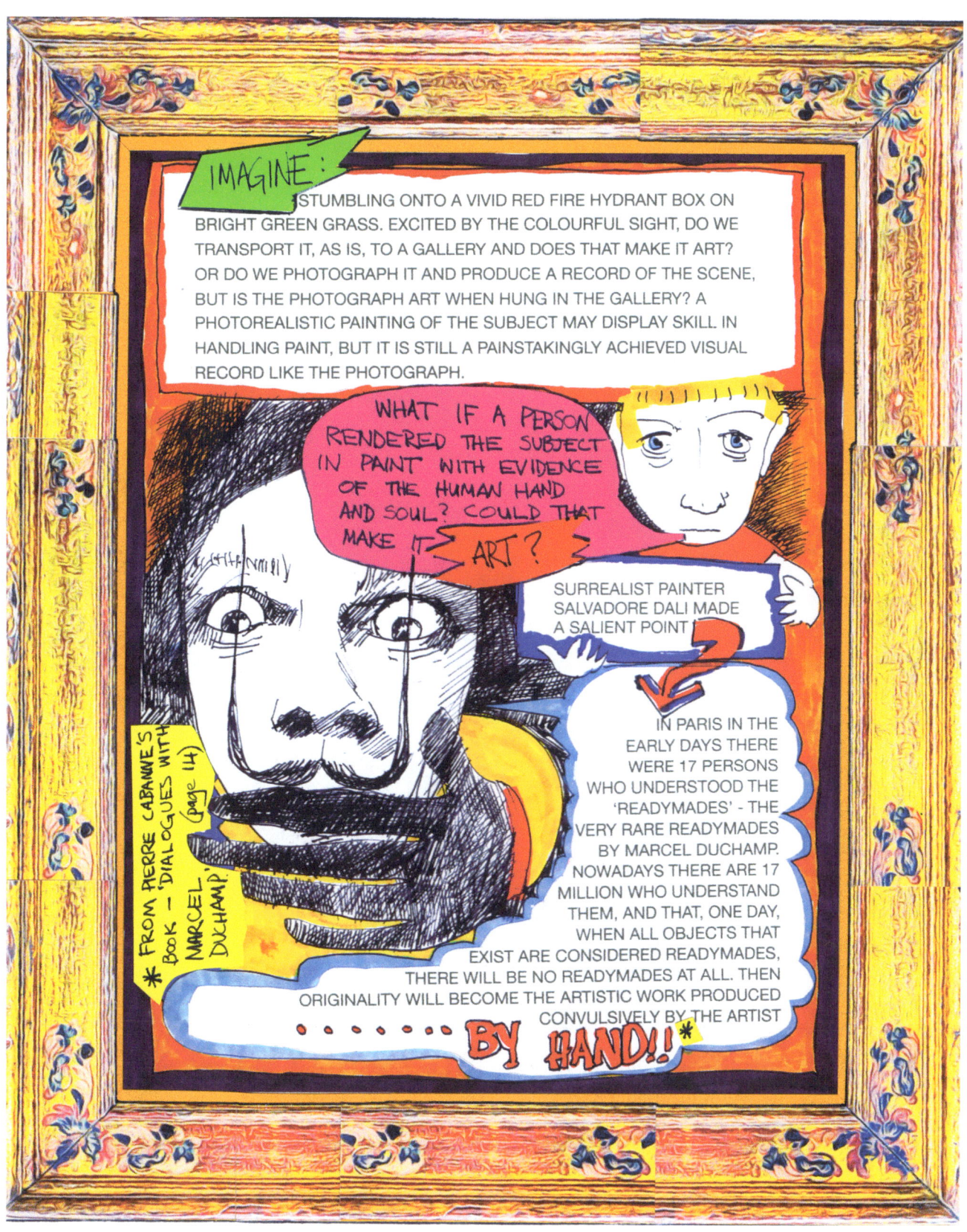

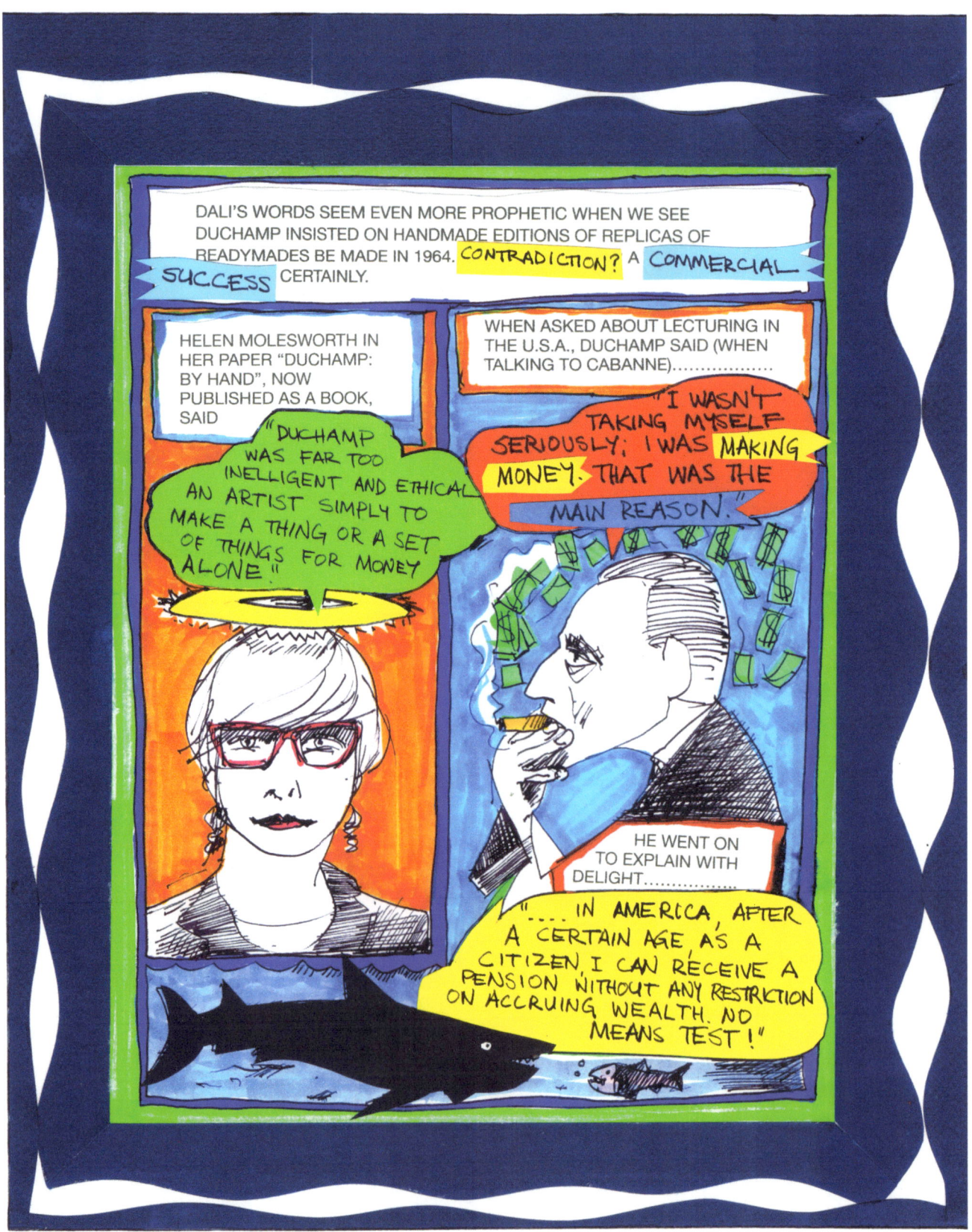

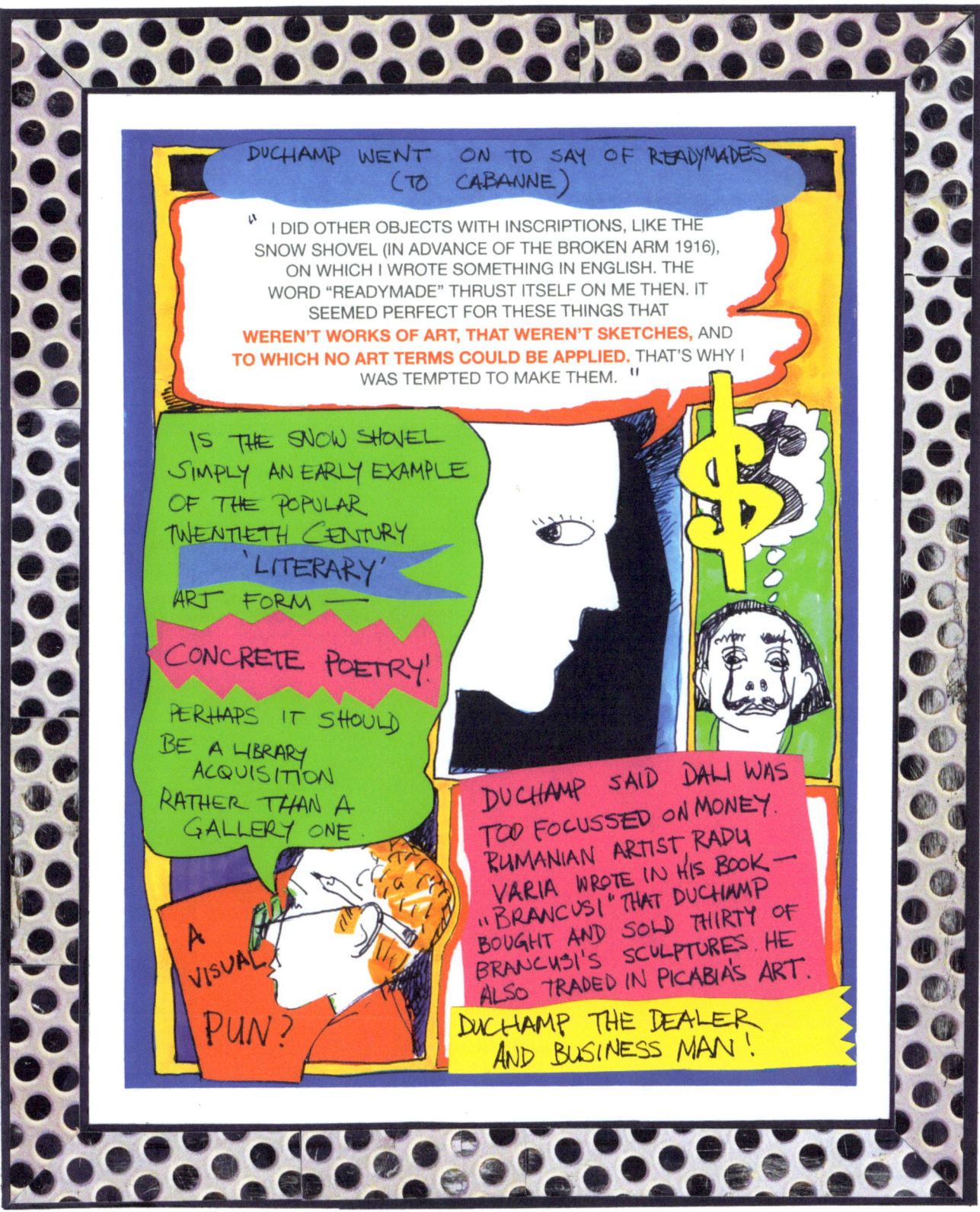

DUCHAMP WENT ON TO SAY OF READYMADES (TO CABANNE)

" I DID OTHER OBJECTS WITH INSCRIPTIONS, LIKE THE SNOW SHOVEL (IN ADVANCE OF THE BROKEN ARM 1916), ON WHICH I WROTE SOMETHING IN ENGLISH. THE WORD "READYMADE" THRUST ITSELF ON ME THEN. IT SEEMED PERFECT FOR THESE THINGS THAT **WEREN'T WORKS OF ART, THAT WEREN'T SKETCHES,** AND **TO WHICH NO ART TERMS COULD BE APPLIED.** THAT'S WHY I WAS TEMPTED TO MAKE THEM. "

IS THE SNOW SHOVEL SIMPLY AN EARLY EXAMPLE OF THE POPULAR TWENTIETH CENTURY 'LITERARY' ART FORM —

CONCRETE POETRY!

PERHAPS IT SHOULD BE A LIBRARY ACQUISITION RATHER THAN A GALLERY ONE

A VISUAL PUN?

DUCHAMP SAID DALI WAS TOO FOCUSSED ON MONEY. RUMANIAN ARTIST, RADU VARIA WROTE IN HIS BOOK — "BRANCUSI" THAT DUCHAMP BOUGHT AND SOLD THIRTY OF BRANCUSI'S SCULPTURES. HE ALSO TRADED IN PICABIA'S ART.

DUCHAMP THE DEALER AND BUSINESS MAN !

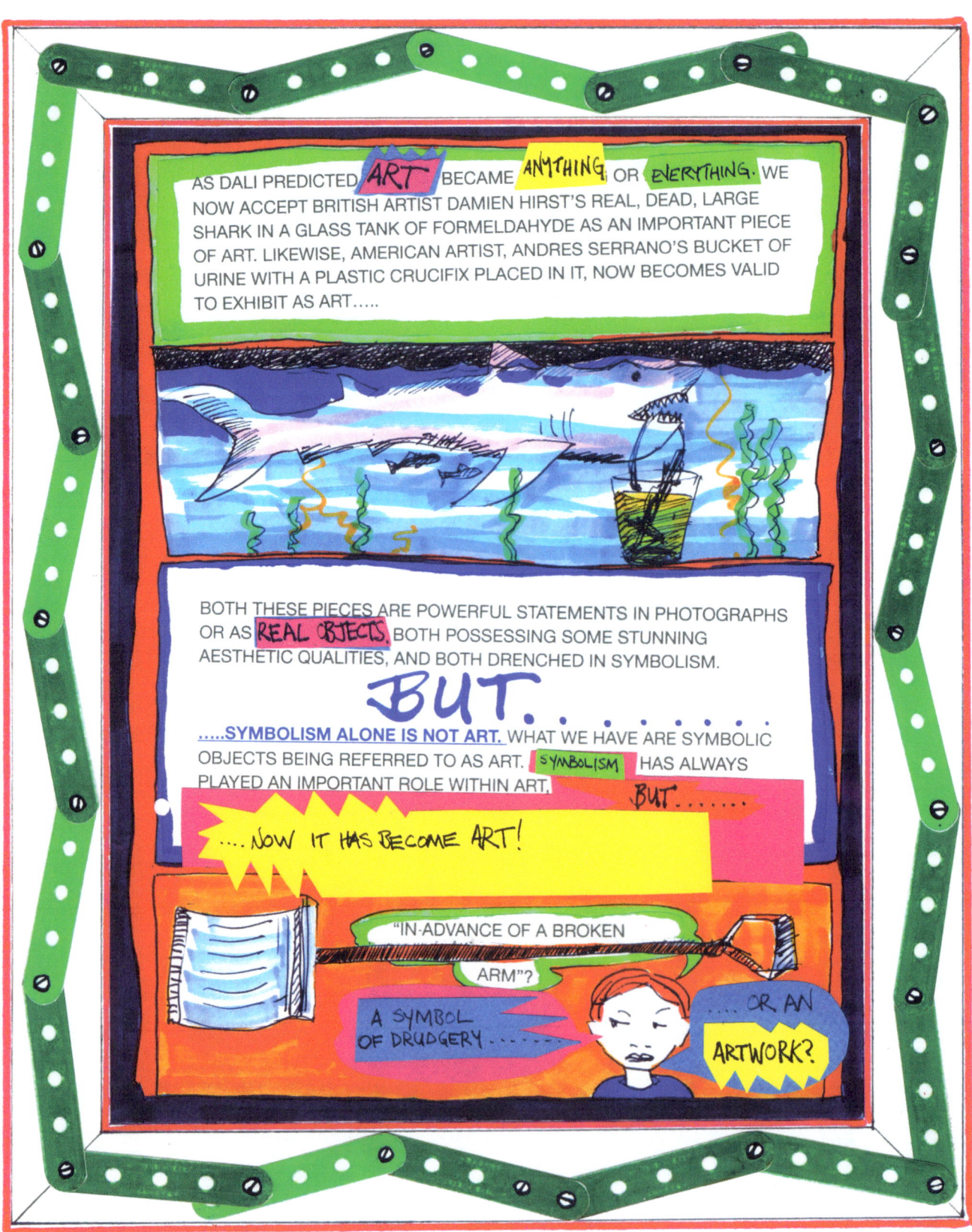

AS DALI PREDICTED **ART** BECAME **ANYTHING**, OR **EVERYTHING**. WE NOW ACCEPT BRITISH ARTIST DAMIEN HIRST'S REAL, DEAD, LARGE SHARK IN A GLASS TANK OF FORMELDAHYDE AS AN IMPORTANT PIECE OF ART. LIKEWISE, AMERICAN ARTIST, ANDRES SERRANO'S BUCKET OF URINE WITH A PLASTIC CRUCIFIX PLACED IN IT, NOW BECOMES VALID TO EXHIBIT AS ART.....

BOTH THESE PIECES ARE POWERFUL STATEMENTS IN PHOTOGRAPHS OR AS **REAL OBJECTS,** BOTH POSSESSING SOME STUNNING AESTHETIC QUALITIES, AND BOTH DRENCHED IN SYMBOLISM.

BUT. . . . .

.....**SYMBOLISM ALONE IS NOT ART.** WHAT WE HAVE ARE SYMBOLIC OBJECTS BEING REFERRED TO AS ART. **SYMBOLISM** HAS ALWAYS PLAYED AN IMPORTANT ROLE WITHIN ART, **BUT........**

....NOW IT HAS BECOME ART!

"IN-ADVANCE OF A BROKEN ARM"?

A SYMBOL OF DRUDGERY.......

.....OR AN ARTWORK?

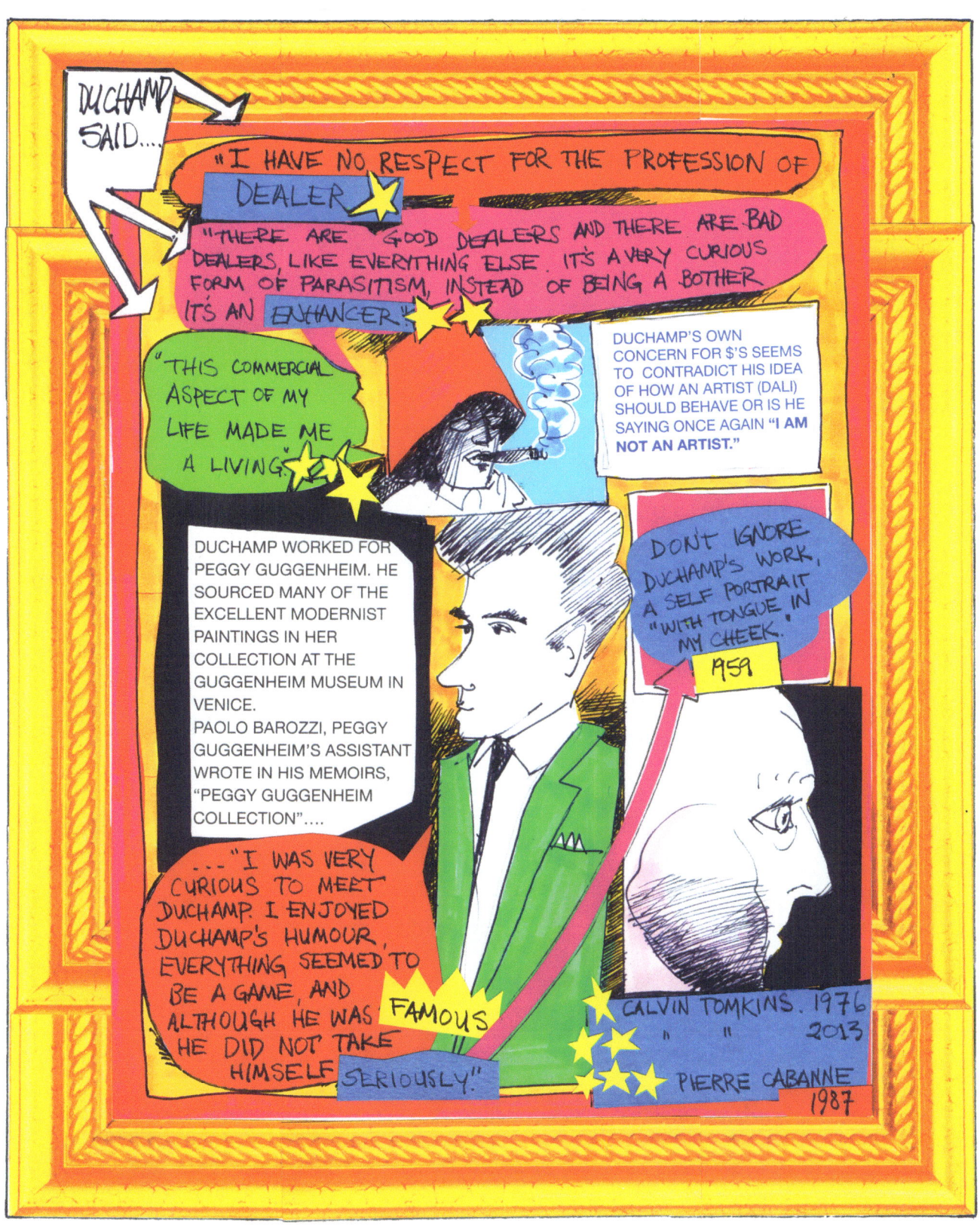

DUCHAMP SAID....

"I HAVE NO RESPECT FOR THE PROFESSION OF DEALER"

"THERE ARE GOOD DEALERS AND THERE ARE BAD DEALERS, LIKE EVERYTHING ELSE. IT'S A VERY CURIOUS FORM OF PARASITISM, INSTEAD OF BEING A BOTHER IT'S AN ENHANCER"

"THIS COMMERCIAL ASPECT OF MY LIFE MADE ME A LIVING"

DUCHAMP'S OWN CONCERN FOR $'S SEEMS TO CONTRADICT HIS IDEA OF HOW AN ARTIST (DALI) SHOULD BEHAVE OR IS HE SAYING ONCE AGAIN "I AM NOT AN ARTIST."

DUCHAMP WORKED FOR PEGGY GUGGENHEIM. HE SOURCED MANY OF THE EXCELLENT MODERNIST PAINTINGS IN HER COLLECTION AT THE GUGGENHEIM MUSEUM IN VENICE.
PAOLO BAROZZI, PEGGY GUGGENHEIM'S ASSISTANT WROTE IN HIS MEMOIRS, "PEGGY GUGGENHEIM COLLECTION"....

DON'T IGNORE DUCHAMP'S WORK, A SELF PORTRAIT "WITH TONGUE IN MY CHEEK." 1959

...."I WAS VERY CURIOUS TO MEET DUCHAMP. I ENJOYED DUCHAMP'S HUMOUR, EVERYTHING SEEMED TO BE A GAME, AND ALTHOUGH HE WAS FAMOUS HE DID NOT TAKE HIMSELF SERIOUSLY."

CALVIN TOMKINS. 1976
"   "   2013

PIERRE CABANNE 1987

13

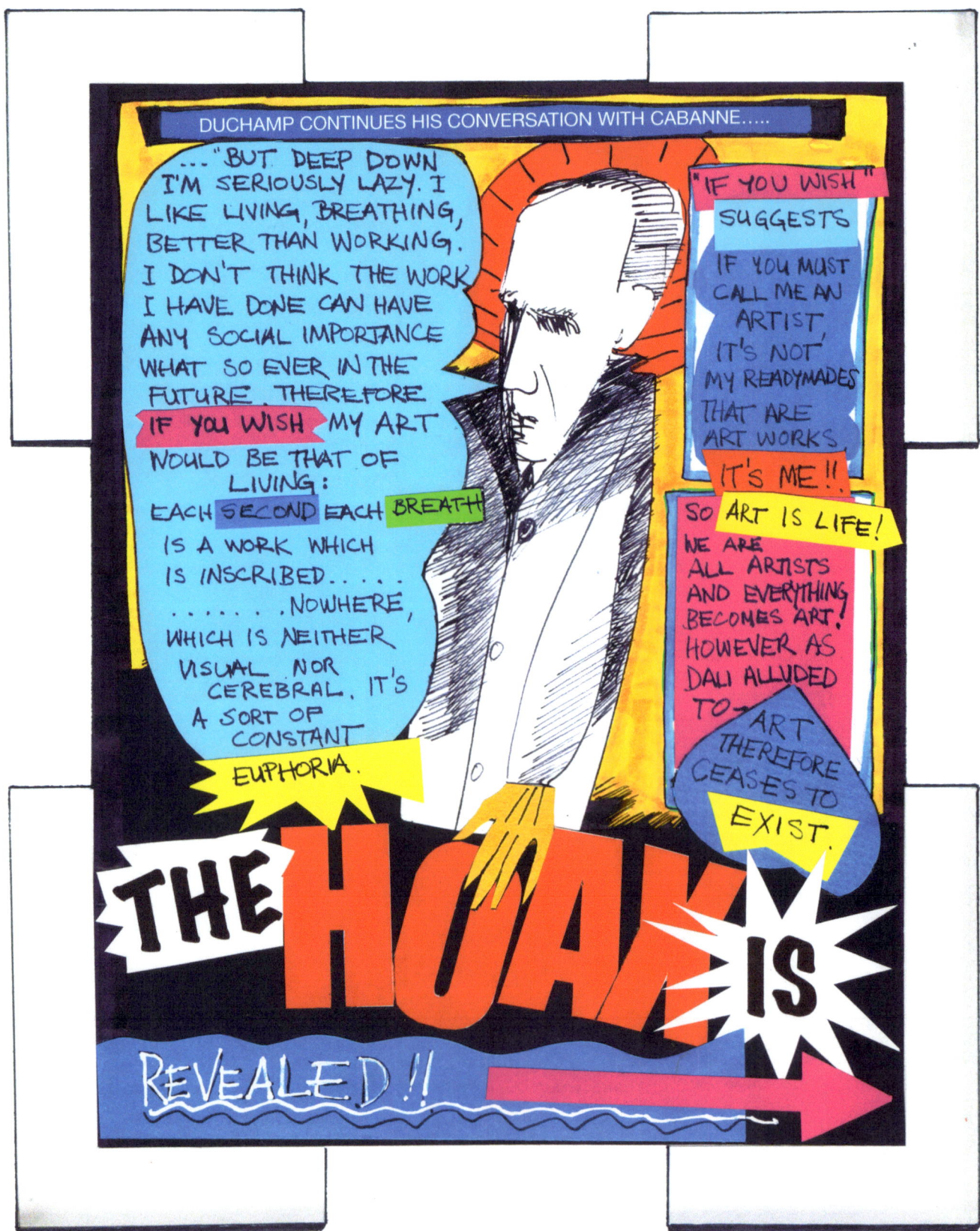

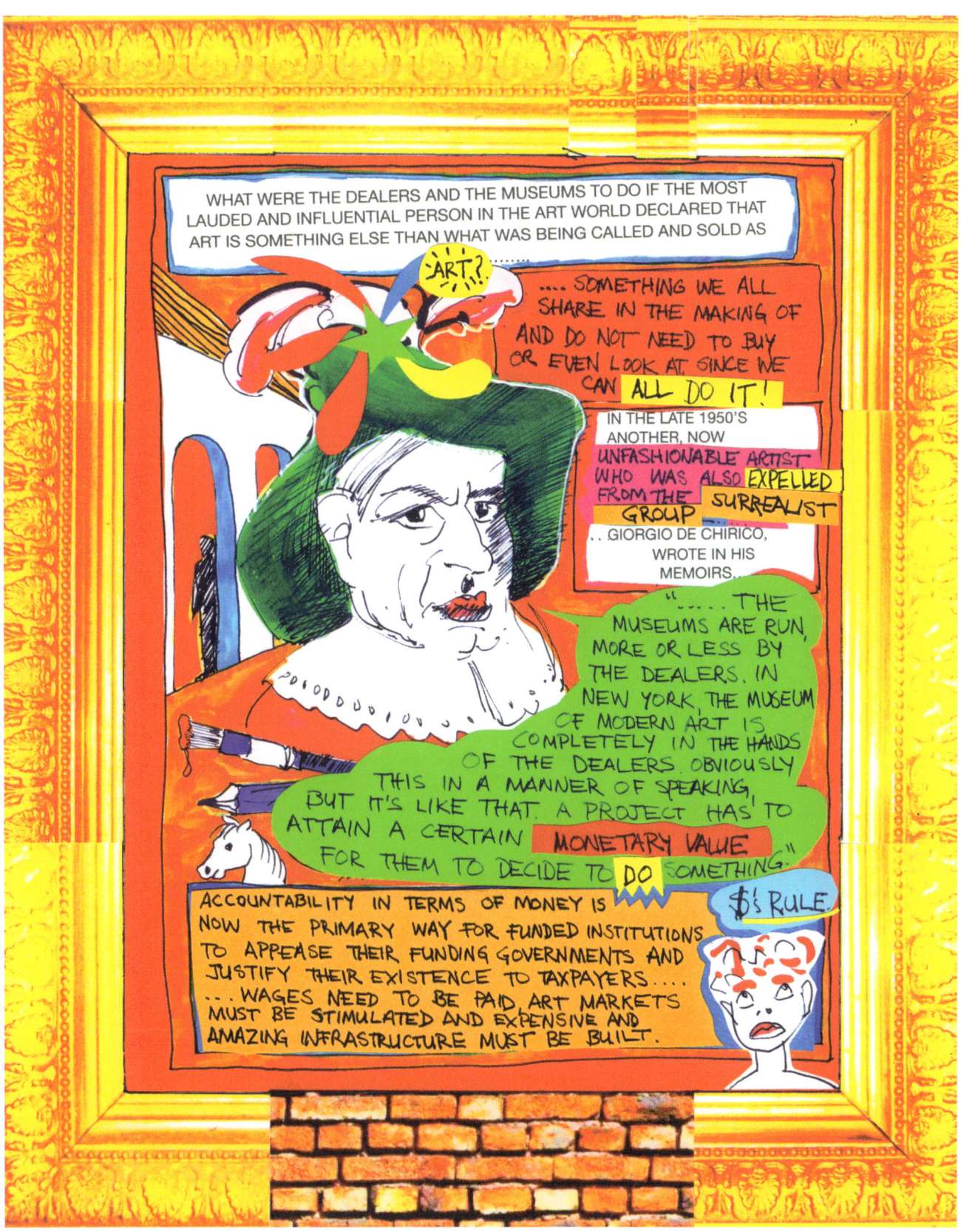

WHAT WERE THE DEALERS AND THE MUSEUMS TO DO IF THE MOST LAUDED AND INFLUENTIAL PERSON IN THE ART WORLD DECLARED THAT ART IS SOMETHING ELSE THAN WHAT WAS BEING CALLED AND SOLD AS

ART.?

..... SOMETHING WE ALL SHARE IN THE MAKING OF AND DO NOT NEED TO BUY OR EVEN LOOK AT, SINCE WE CAN ALL DO IT!

IN THE LATE 1950'S ANOTHER, NOW UNFASHIONABLE ARTIST WHO WAS ALSO EXPELLED FROM THE SURREALIST GROUP

... GIORGIO DE CHIRICO, WROTE IN HIS MEMOIRS...

".....THE MUSEUMS ARE RUN, MORE OR LESS BY THE DEALERS. IN NEW YORK, THE MUSEUM OF MODERN ART IS COMPLETELY IN THE HANDS OF THE DEALERS. OBVIOUSLY THIS IN A MANNER OF SPEAKING, BUT IT'S LIKE THAT. A PROJECT HAS TO ATTAIN A CERTAIN MONETARY VALUE FOR THEM TO DECIDE TO DO SOMETHING."

$'s RULE

ACCOUNTABILITY IN TERMS OF MONEY IS NOW THE PRIMARY WAY FOR FUNDED INSTITUTIONS TO APPEASE THEIR FUNDING GOVERNMENTS AND JUSTIFY THEIR EXISTENCE TO TAXPAYERS....
... WAGES NEED TO BE PAID, ART MARKETS MUST BE STIMULATED AND EXPENSIVE AND AMAZING INFRASTRUCTURE MUST BE BUILT.

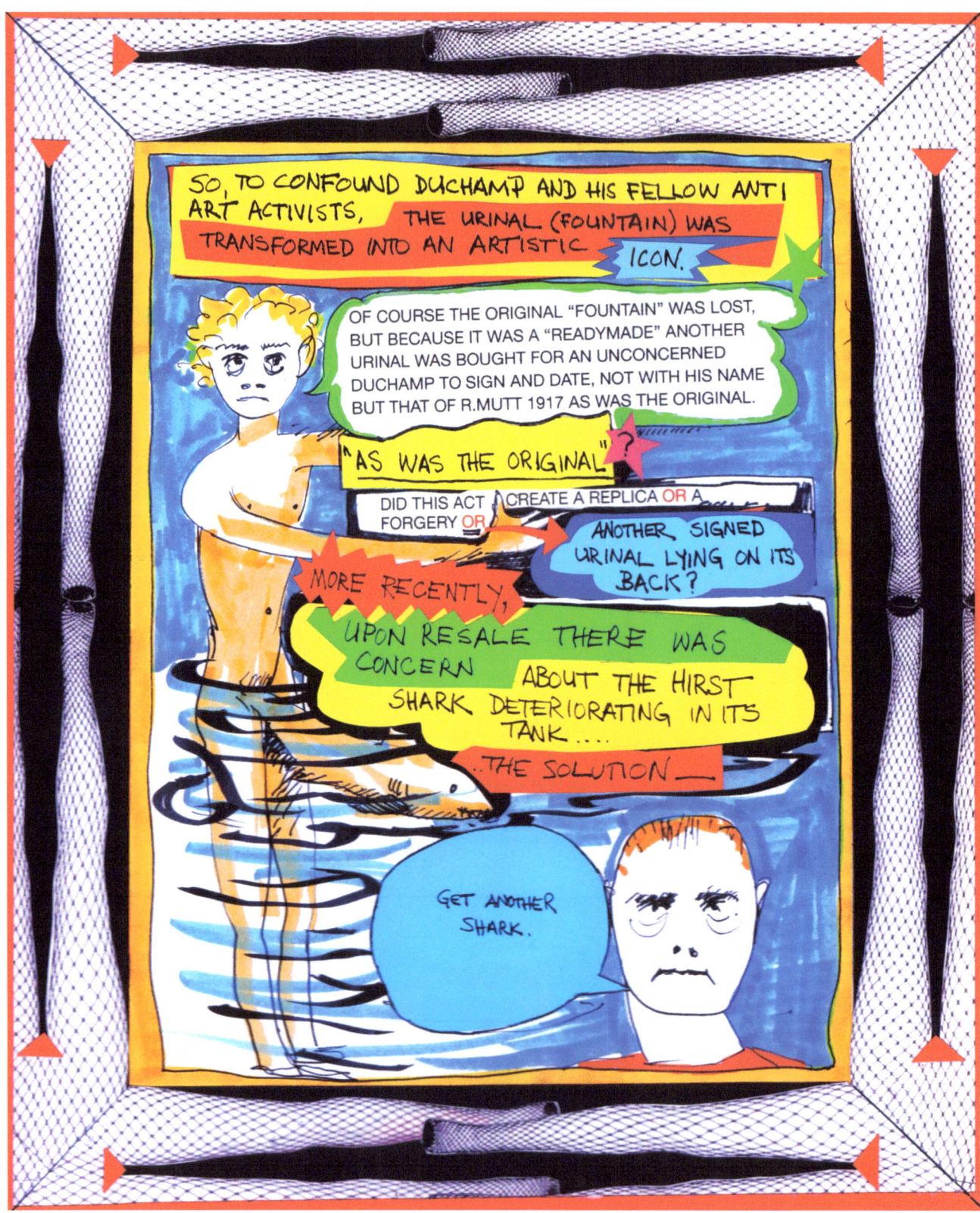

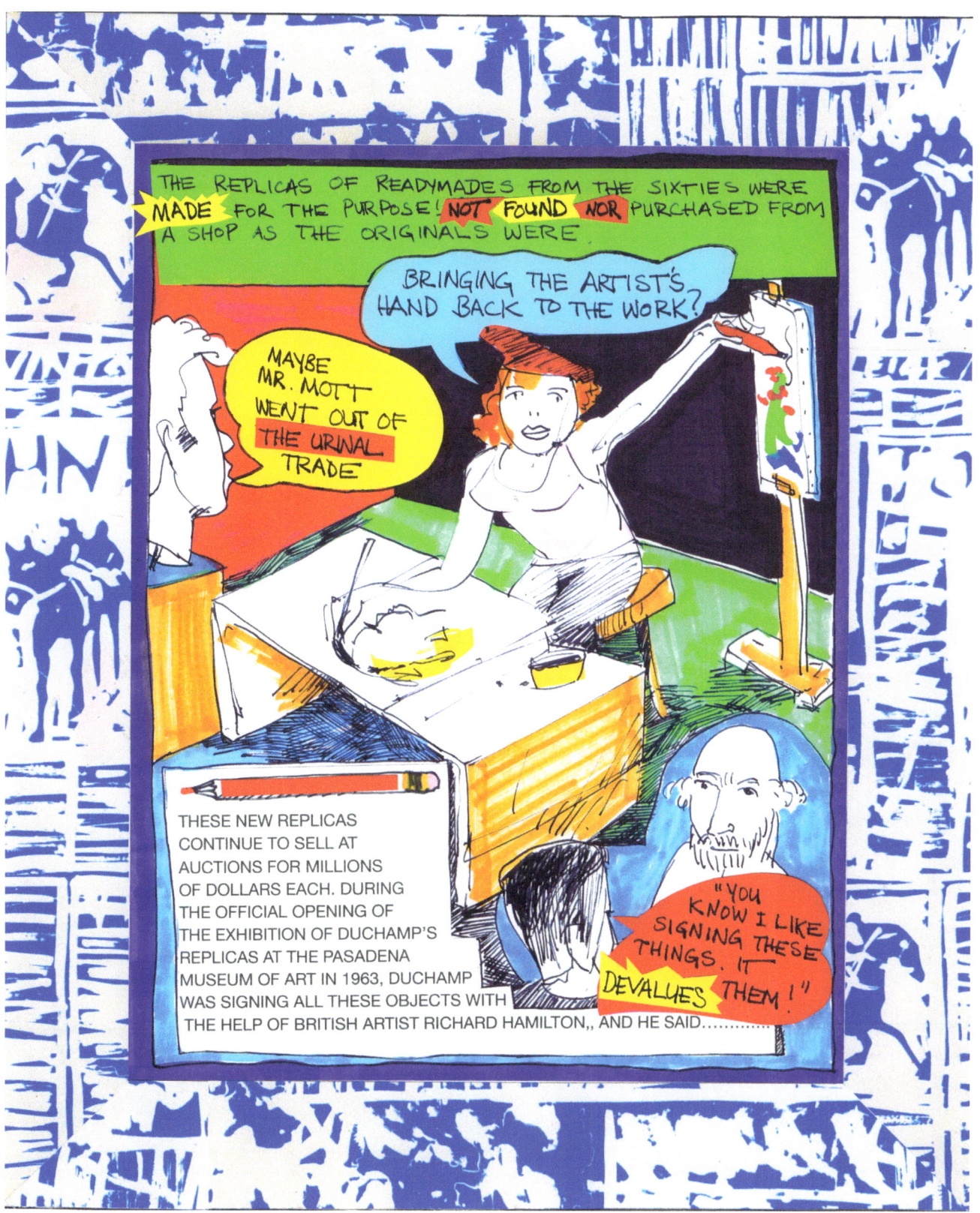

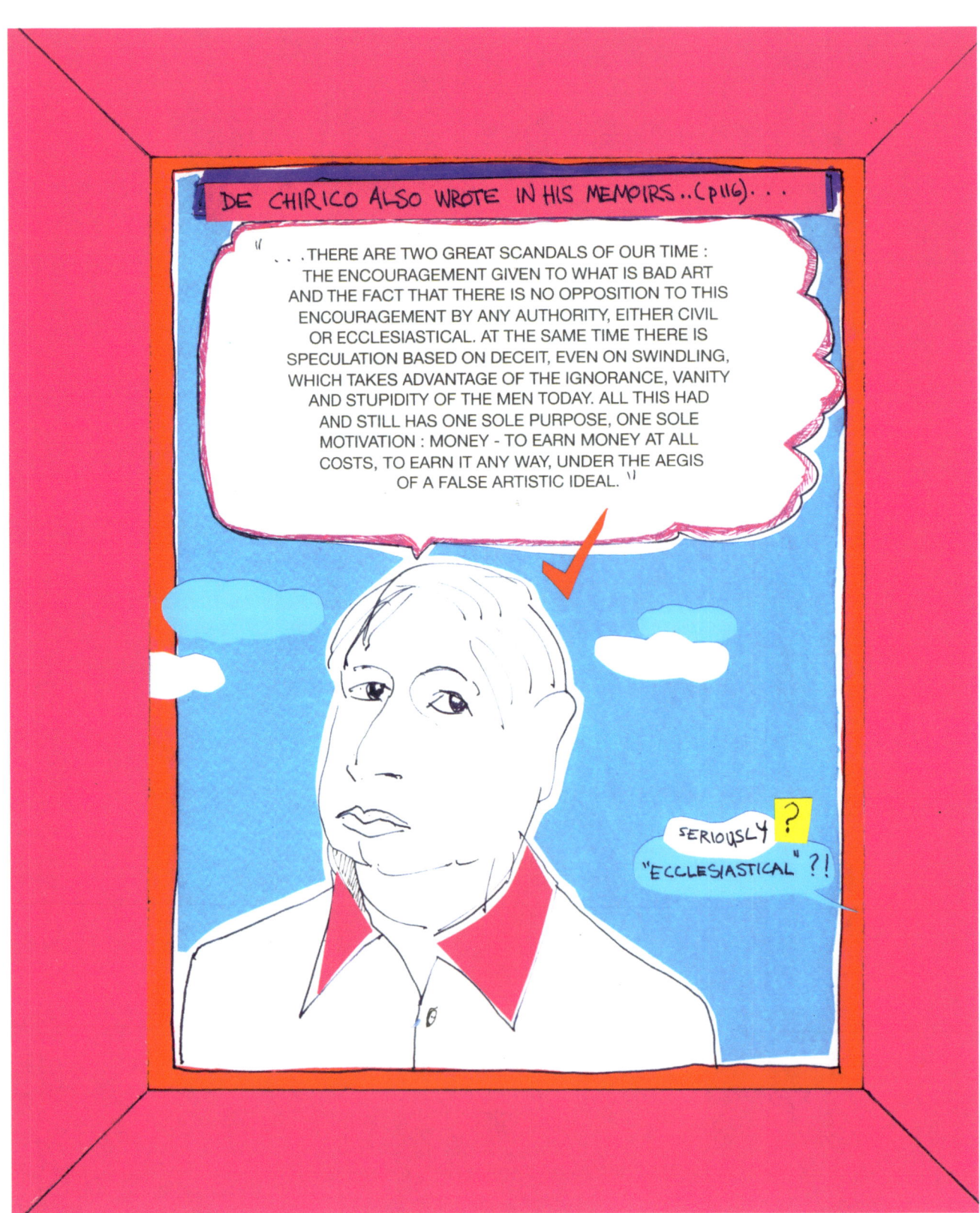

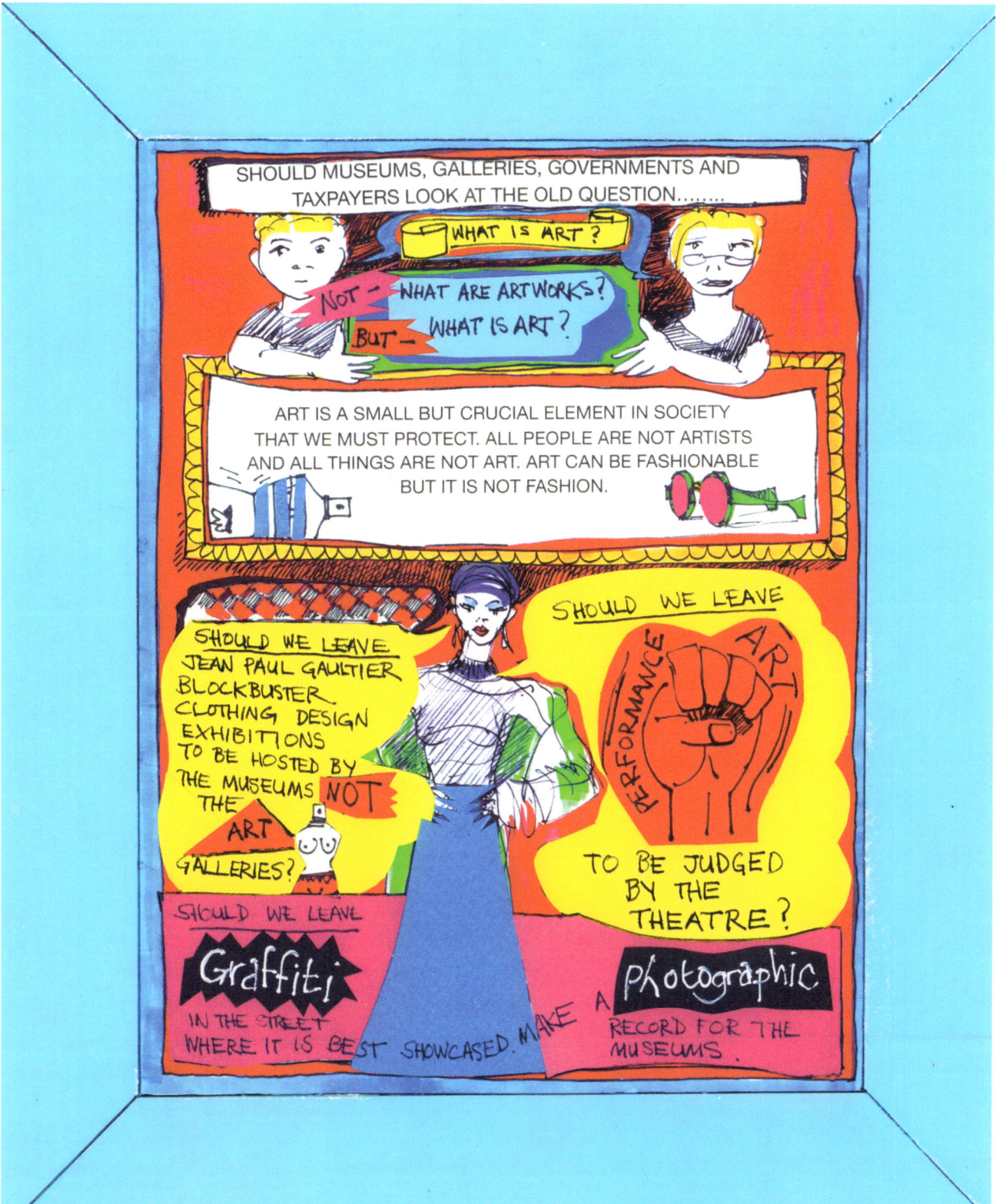

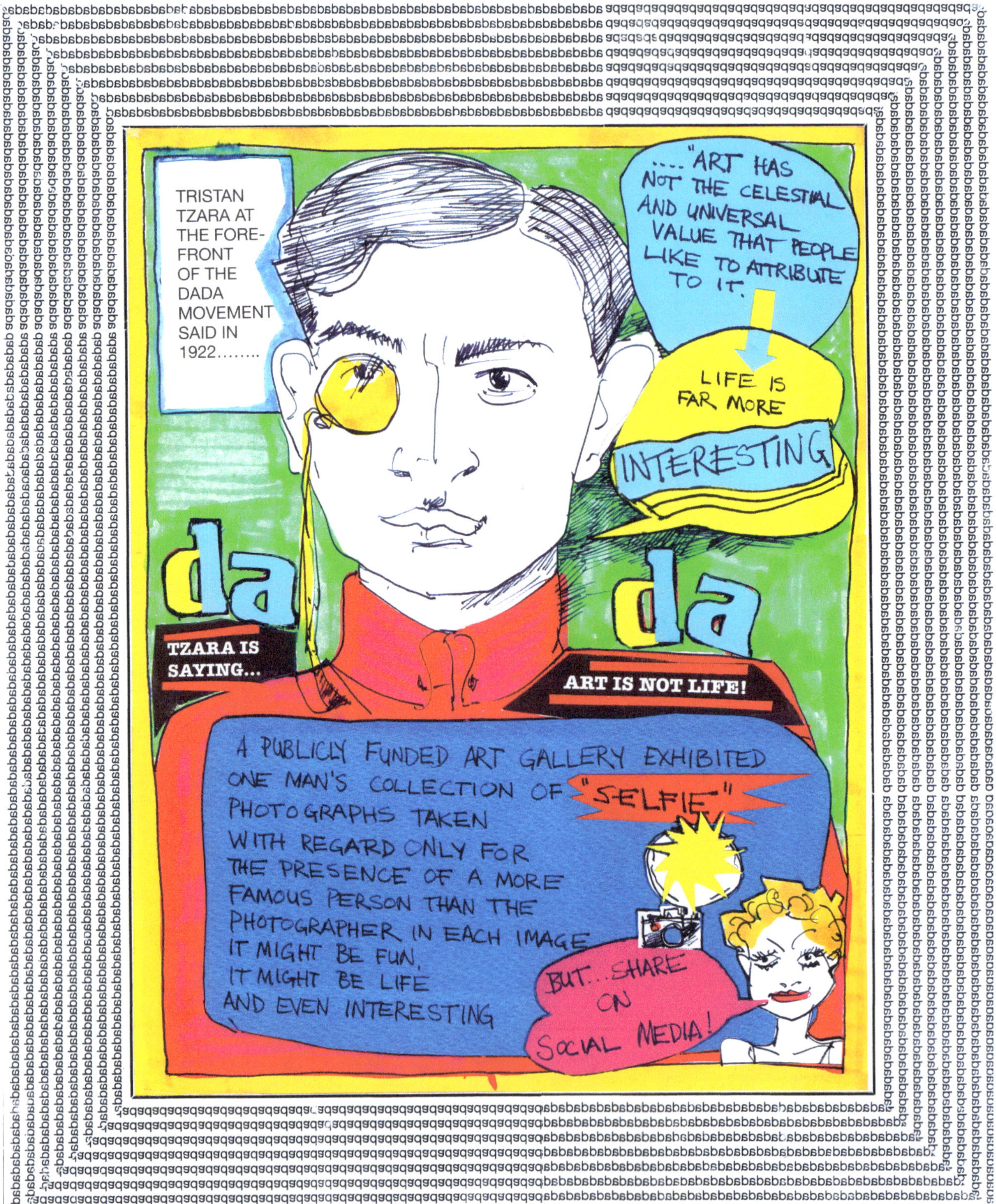

TRISTAN TZARA AT THE FORE-FRONT OF THE DADA MOVEMENT SAID IN 1922……..
…."ART HAS NOT THE CELESTIAL AND UNIVERSAL VALUE THAT PEOPLE LIKE TO ATTRIBUTE TO IT.
LIFE IS FAR MORE INTERESTING
da
da
TZARA IS SAYING...
ART IS NOT LIFE!
A PUBLICLY FUNDED ART GALLERY EXHIBITED ONE MAN'S COLLECTION OF "SELFIE" PHOTOGRAPHS TAKEN WITH REGARD ONLY FOR THE PRESENCE OF A MORE FAMOUS PERSON THAN THE PHOTOGRAPHER IN EACH IMAGE IT MIGHT BE FUN, IT MIGHT BE LIFE AND EVEN INTERESTING
BUT...SHARE ON SOCIAL MEDIA!

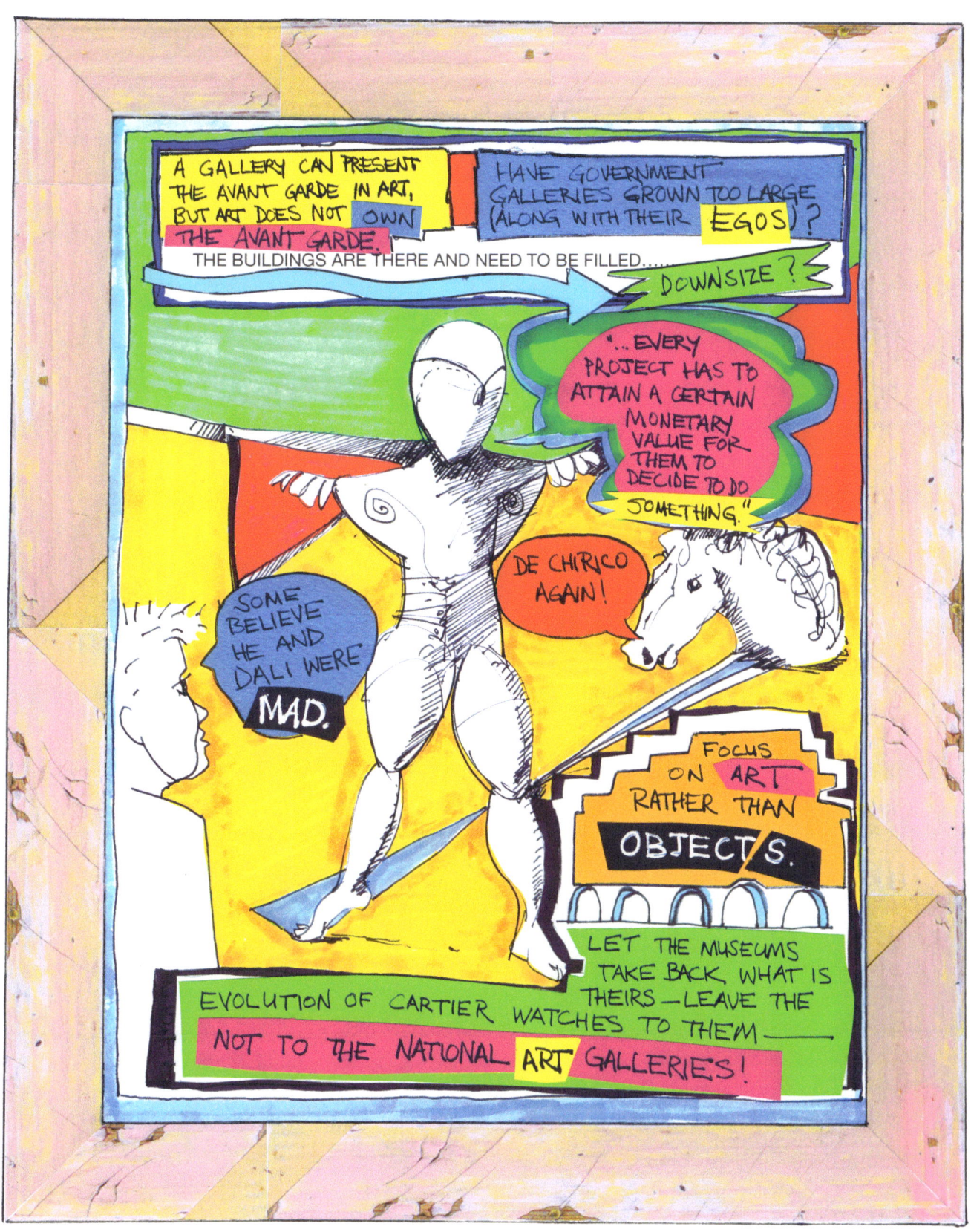

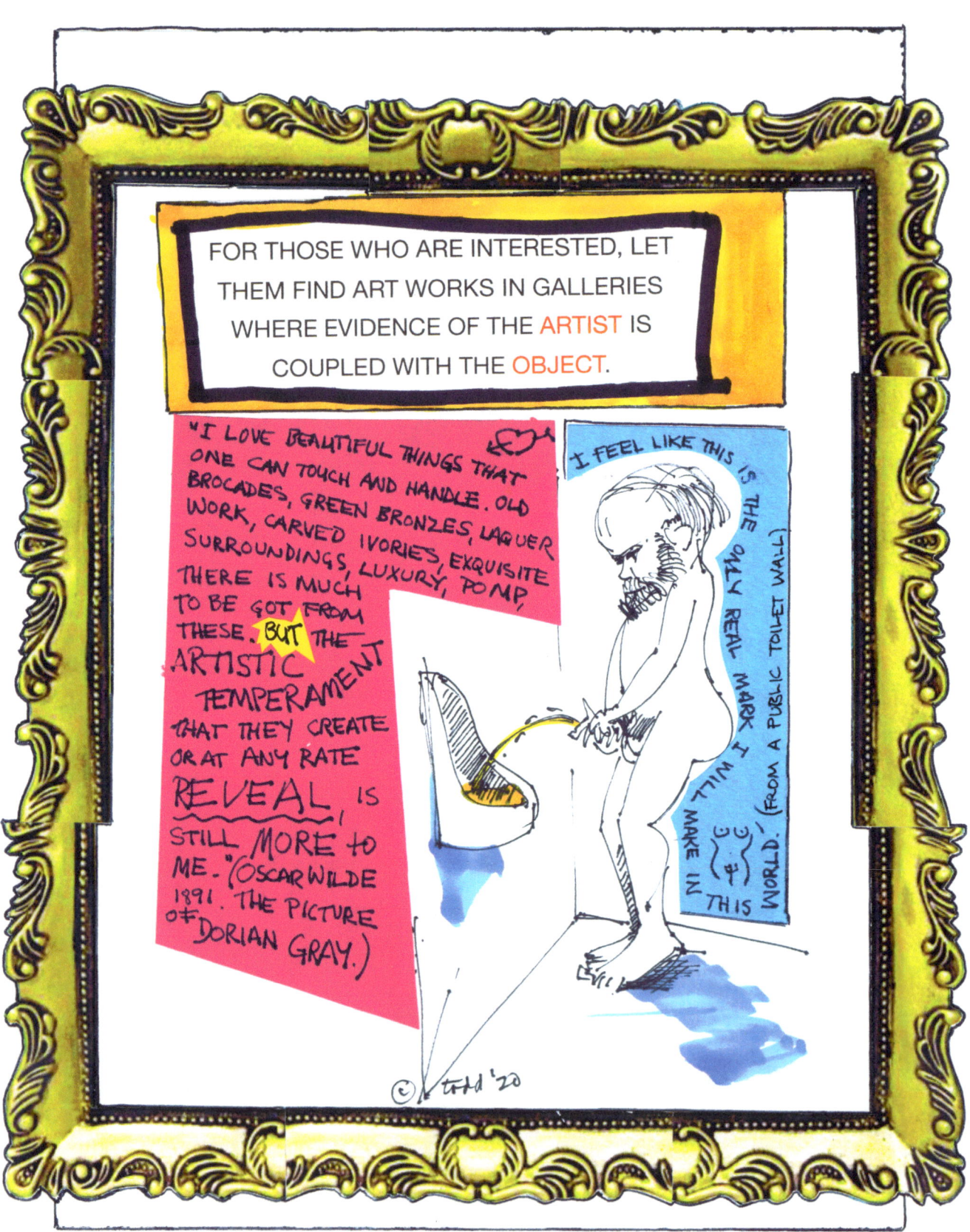

FOR THOSE WHO ARE INTERESTED, LET THEM FIND ART WORKS IN GALLERIES WHERE EVIDENCE OF THE ARTIST IS COUPLED WITH THE OBJECT.

"I LOVE BEAUTIFUL THINGS THAT ONE CAN TOUCH AND HANDLE. OLD BROCADES, GREEN BRONZES, LAQUER WORK, CARVED IVORIES, EXQUISITE SURROUNDINGS, LUXURY, POMP, THERE IS MUCH TO BE GOT FROM THESE. BUT THE ARTISTIC TEMPERAMENT THAT THEY CREATE OR AT ANY RATE REVEAL, IS STILL MORE TO ME." (OSCAR WILDE 1891. THE PICTURE OF DORIAN GRAY.)

I FEEL LIKE THIS IS THE ONLY REAL MARK I WILL MAKE IN THIS WORLD." (FROM A PUBLIC TOILET WALL)